RED WING
COLLECTIBLES

Dan DePasquale
Gail DePasquale
Larry Peterson

COLLECTOR BOOKS
A Division of Schroeder Publishing Co., Inc.

Searching For A Publisher?

We are always looking for knowledgeable people considered to be experts within their fields. If you feel that there is a real need for a book on your collectible subject and have a large comprehensive collection, contact us.

COLLECTOR BOOKS
P.O. Box 3009
Paducah, Kentucky 42002-3009

Additional copies of this book may be ordered from

COLLECTOR BOOKS
P.O. Box 3009
Paducah, Kentucky 42002-3009

@ $9.95. Add $2.00 for postage and handling.

Printed by IMAGE GRAPHICS, INC., Paducah, Kentucky

Acknowledgments

A book of this nature can never be published without the help and support of others. We would like to recognize Ray Pahnke and Dave Kuffel from Chicago; Dennis Yaeggi from Wisconsin; and Con and Sandy Short from North Dakota, for sending photos from their areas and/or collections. Another "thank you" goes to Bonnie and Gary Tefft for their assistance and the use of a photo from their book, *Red Wing Potters and Their Wares*.

Others gave encouragement, photos and/or allowed us to photograph their collections. These friendships and sharing attitudes are what collecting is all about.

California
Bill Gore
Mike and Russa Robinson
Illinois
Dave Kuffel
Steve Manning
Bob and Edna Marker
Jim and Patti Martin
Chuck and Darlene McDaniel
Ray and Nadine Pahnke
Taugie and Beth Slaith
Iowa
Larry and Pat Ambler
George and Rosie Boggess
Dick and Elaine Fastenau
Doug and Diane Lanning
Richard and Frances Larsen
Kansas
Richard Cronemeyer
Don and Eleanor Denney
Jr. and Jan Denney
Ron and Marilyn Richardson
Minnesota
Morris and Delores Callstrom
Mr. and Mrs. Harry Casa
Mary Costello
Jean Donovan
Chuck and Eva Drometer
Bob and Joanne Hagen
Royce and Vi Malmquist

Henry and Evelyn Mayer
Cecil and Rachel Morris
Ernie and Colleen Nelson
Jim Norine
Rich and Bonnie Peters
Bob and Jewell Peterson
Pat Ray
Steve and Phyllis Showers
Jack and Mary Lou Valek
Roland and Bev Winchell
Steve Wipperling
Missouri
Henry Heflin
Dean Johnson
Jack Woods
Nebraska
Duane and Nan Baker
Ron and Robin Hruska
Pat and Mary McGilvrey
Steve and Marty Okeson
Lonnie and Donna Spies
North Dakota
Con and Sandy Short
Wisconsin
Llyod and Vera Hutchinson
Gary and Bonnie Tefft
Lyndon Viel
Dennis Welt
Warren Wood
Dennis and Nona Yaeggi

Important Dates in the History of Red Wing, Minnesota's Clay Industry

1. Red Wing Stoneware Company, 1877–1906
2. Minnesota Stoneware Company, 1883–1906
3. North Star Stoneware Company, 1892–1896
4. Union Stoneware Company, 1894–1906
   (The joining of the three stoneware companies for economic efficiency; each retained their own identity, however.)
5. Red Wing Union Stoneware Company, 1906–1936
   (The remaining two companies, Red Wing and Minnesota, united to form one new company.)
6. Red Wing Potteries, 1936–1967

Value Guide

A definitive value for any particular piece does not exist. The accompanying prices in this book are only guides intended to help a buyer determine an approximate measure of value. The value of advertising ware is even more subjective since individual interest and location become important buying factors. Additionally, prices for miniature jugs seem to be in a state of flux and, as yet, have not stabilized. Many readers may have purchased some items illustrated for much less or for much more. Keep in mind that condition, company mark, size, rarity and desirability all help determine value; but, in the final analysis, the value of a particular piece is worth only what a particular buyer is willing to pay.

The range of value given on an item assumes that the piece is in mint condition even though the item illustrated may not be. If the item shown is marked on the bottom or side wall it will be indicated by a code placed in parentheses; e.g., (RW1) which refers to the marking section in Chapter V. For a similar item to be of the same value, it also must be marked; though, generally, it does not have to be the exact same mark.

Table of Contents

Introduction

As emphasized in our first book, *Red Wing Stoneware,* literally hundreds of types and styles of items were produced first by the stoneware companies located in Red Wing, Minnesota, and then, later, by Red Wing Potteries. For ninety years (1877–1967) Red Wing, Minnesota, was the self-proclaimed pottery capital of America. This long, proud and prolific history is one reason that Red Wing collecting is such a popular hobby today. The uniqueness and variety of the products produced provide something for everyone.

The success of Red Wing Stoneware as a comprehensive overview of the general product lines made by the various stoneware companies in Red Wing has led to this companion volume. Red Wing collectors have expanded their collections and their interests to include areas only briefly discussed in Chapter III of Red Wing Stoneware. The focus of that chapter and of this book is on specializing.

Why Specialize?

Most Red Wing collectors begin with the idea in mind of collecting one of every item the companies produced. They soon learn that because of lack of space and/or availability of funds that they somehow have to limit their collecting. Also, as the scope of their experience broadens, they find that certain items seem to have more personal appeal than others, depending on their individual interests. New and old collectors alike, therefore, can enjoy the rewards that specializing brings. The sheer number and variety of products made by the "pot shops," as they were referred to by the locals, allow for the diversity of individual collecting tastes and personalities. An additional benefit of specializing is that it provides the challenge of pursuing a subject in depth.

Some obvious specializing possibilities open to collectors of Red Wing stoneware might include the following:

1. by Decoration

2. by Sets

3. by Color

Innumerable possibilities exist for each of the aforementioned categories. *Red Wing Stoneware* is an excellent source for choosing a product line specialty area.

Red Wing Collectibles will explore additional specialty options open to collectors of Red Wing products — be they collectors of stoneware or pottery or both. A major portion of the book is devoted to advertising ware, since it is fast becoming one of the leading collectible specialty areas for devotees of Red Wing products. One reason for this is that it is all encompassing — both in terms of the range of products made and in its regional and personal appeal depending on the advertising displayed. Likewise, the collecting of miniature jugs is very popular today. Their small size not only gives them a special charm but it also allows for easier home display possibilities. The rest of the book is devoted to additional options for specializing — from sewer pipe samples to dinnerware. The choices are endless and exciting. Enjoy.

CHAPTER I: ADVERTISING

Retailing is and was a competitive business. Therefore, it was as important for the merchant of the past to have an "edge" over his competition as it is today. Old stoneware catalogs offered many styles and colors of advertising from which a progressive and enterprising businessman could choose to promote his business and/or product.

We Make a Specialty of Underglaze Stamping.

Stamping in Blue, Black, Brown or Green.

This page from a turn-of-the-century Union Stoneware catalog illustrates examples of advertising logos that were actually used by various companies. The liquor and creamery industries were the two biggest purchasers of early advertising ware. Most of these older advertising pieces listed only the name of the store, the product sold, and the location of the store. The customer merely purchased the product itself and received the container free. Although "stamping in blue, black, brown, or green" is advertised, we have never seen examples of the latter two colors. Look for examples of these same advertising logos on actual jugs and butter crocks pictured elsewhere in the book.

Later advertising pieces may have been unrelated to the tpye of business advertised; rather, they served as promotional items or as "give aways" to preferred customers in order to promote the business itself instead of a particular product.

This pitcher from the popular spongeband line made in the 1930's is a prime example of just such a piece. It was important that the item given away be one that the customer would use often so that the item itself would serve as a constant reminder of the merchant's generosity. Kitchenware served this purpose perfectly.

Advertising items have always held a special charm and fascination for Red Wing collectors. One reason for their popularity is that they can provide a wealth of information about the Red Wing companies and their products.

Marketing areas can be determined from the various towns and states mentioned in the ads. Red Wing products were shipped by rail over a large area of the United States. Advertising examples shown in this chapter indicate that the scope of their selling territory extended from the eastern U.S. to Canada to Texas to California. Approximate age determinant of various product lines is another advantage of advertising logos if they include the year the item was given away. This is especially important since most known old catalogs were undated.

Still another advantage of collecting advertising pieces is that one has the opportunity to acquire either a sampling of almost every type of item the Red Wing companies produced or he can again specialize in a particular product line. A study of advertising pieces is therefore, in reality, a study of pieces manufactured throughout the companies' histories.

These Nebraska advertising pieces illustrate the extensive variety of products used for advertising purposes. They also prove the success of the salesman (men) Red Wing had in Nebraska.

By far the most personal touch that advertising items afford the collector is to display the collector's name. Lucky are the people whose name is Peterson.

PRODUCT LINES: JUGS

To describe this piece as merely being "rare" is like saying that the Grand Canyon is simply "big." Suffice it to say that this 15 gallon, double-handled, hand-turned, sidewall-stamped, salt-glazed jug with blue stenciled letters advertising Red Wing Stoneware Co. products is among the ultimate in Red Wing collecting treasures. Regnier and Shoup Crockery Co. in St. Joseph, Missouri, either commissioned the Red Wing Stoneware Co. in the 1880's to make this piece in order to help sell their products or the stoneware company itself gave it to them for being such a good customer.

Glenwood and Inglewood were Minneapolis competitors until 1896 when they joined. The jug on the left, therefore, predates the one on the right. Red Wing dump shards prove their maker's verification. Interestingly enough, the Glenwood-Inglewood Co. still operates today. 2 gal. (both unsigned) $350.00-450.00 ea.

Dark blue stenciling adds even further beauty to this fine example of a salt glaze beehive jug. This company was located in Minneapolis from 1891 to 1910, and this must have been one of their earliest containers. 2 gal. (unsigned) $400.00-500.00.

Though not signed with the company maker, there is no doubt as to the Dubuque, Iowa, jug's authenticity. It was literally dug from the old stoneware companies' dump by an experienced "digger." Not only the stenciling but also the bottom marking add to the value of the jug on the right. L. 1 gal. (unsigned) $400.00-500.00; R. 1 gal. (M2) $500.00-600.00.

These beautiful bottom-signed glazed jugs would be rare even without advertising. L. 1 gal. (RW 6) $450.00-550.00; R. 2 gal. (RW 4) $450.00-550.00.

The Red Wing stoneware companies were, throughout their history, commissioned by several different companies to make certain one-of-a-kind advertising wares for the purpose of promoting their businesses. These unusual products are different either in color, shape or design from any other pieces manufactured. They will be found with and identifying advertising logo of a particular company only. Instead of selecting from the Red Wing company's suggested products and glazes, they wanted a whole new promotional item. Needless to say, they are in scarce supply today. One such purchaser was Wm. Radam for his "Microbe Killer."

The raised advertising on these normally brown-topped Minnesota and Red Wing Stoneware Co. jugs is unlike any other Red Wing advertising known. "Wm. Radam's Microbe Killer" was a patent medicine which, evidently, was a big seller, as he had seventeen factories scattered across the U.S. in 1890. Jugs in many shapes and styles made by several different companies have been found with a variety of Radam's Microbe Killer advertising logs. Bottom markings become most important, therefore, for company identification. L. 1 gal. (M 3) $350.00-400.00; R. 1 gal. (RW 3) $350.00-400.00.

The unique shapes of these jugs qualify them as special order items. This "medicine" was denounced by the medical community and referred to as "man made pink lightning" since it was mostly water with the addition of a little wine for color. It was manufactured in three different strengths and sold for $3.00 per jug. Both (M 3), $225.00-275.00 ea.

Double handled jugs are exceedingly rare, but this one from Excelsior Springs, Missouri, exhibiting mineral water advertising, is especially unique. 5 gal. $1,500.00-2,000.00.

Colfax, Iowa, was also well known for its mineral springs and spas in the early 1900's. Their use of Red Wing beehive jugs and creative logo designs was second to none as the examples both to the left and below illustrate. 5 gal. $500.00-600.00.

Many hotels, bath houses, sanitariums and spas sold mineral water from springs on their own land — thus the reason for so many different advertising logos. 5 gal. $500.00-600.00.

Until glass bottles came on the market, the Glenwood-Inglewood Co. continued to purchase their containers from Red Wing. This 2 gallon white beehive is perfectly proportioned and is adorned with an attractive logo. One of this company's slogans was "Water your people and watch them grow." 2 gal. (unsigned) $300.00-400.00.

The blue stamping on these jugs provides a stunning contrast to the shiny white glazes. Although these two jugs are both 3 gallons in size, the hand-turning process caused their shapes to be slightly different. 3 gal. $700.00-800.00 ea.

The different advertising styles shown on these 3 gallon beehives provide an interesting contrast. Note, too, the pronounced ridges caused by hand-turning. 3 gal. $400.00-500.00 ea.

These are more fine examples of well-proportioned, hand-turned 5 gallon beehive jugs — their beauty accented with ovals and leaves. They both display unusual liquor advertising logos from Chicago merchants. Notice the interesting lip on the pouring spout and the use of the Union oval on the right hand jug. L. $600.00-700.00; R. $700.00-800.00.

Whereas urban Chicago was known for its multitude of liquor dealers, rural Nebraska in the early 1900's was dominated by stores selling "General Merchandise." Each small town (and most towns were very small) had one store that furnished everything a family could ever need — from "jewelry" to "farm machinery" to which the jug on the bottom right testifies! It is not known, however, what the contents of these jugs were when they were originally sold. Top, L. $600.00-700.00; R. $700.00-800.00; Bottom, L. (M 12) $400.00-500.00; R. $700.00-800.00.

Stoneware beauties such as these displaying Chicago advertising make collectors grateful for the good job achieved by the Red Wing sales representative(s) in the Chicago area during the early 1900's. Notice the dash dot dash under the 4 on the left hand jug – a carry over from the hand decorated salt glaze tradition. 4 gal. $500.00-600.00 ea.

The unusual pouring spout shown on this 3 gallon jug is unique to larger gallonage shoulder jugs displaying Groomes and Ullrich advertising. L. 3 gal. (RWU 1) $250.00-300.00; R. 1 gal. (M 9) $125.00-150.00.

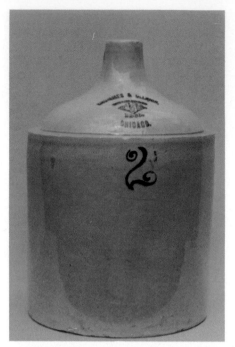

This 2 gallon jug is extraordinary because it is the only 2 gallon Red Wing jug known stamped with a "2". Even though this company's logo can be found on jugs of many different shapes and sizes, its placement was always near the spout (unsigned) $200.00-250.00.

Although wing shoulder jugs are among the most common items Red Wing produced, very few displayed advertising as well as the red wing. Large capacity jugs were ideally suited for mineral water containers. $400.00-500.00 ea.

Another jug advertising mineral water is even more unusual because it displays the Red Wing Union oval as well as a large red wing. 5 gal. $400.00-500.00.

These jugs with Chicago liquor advertising are in the harder-to-find 4 gallon size. Not only does the Many, Blanc and Co. jug on the left give the name of the company president and secretary, but it also boasts of the company's "Three Telephones." $400.00-500.00 ea.

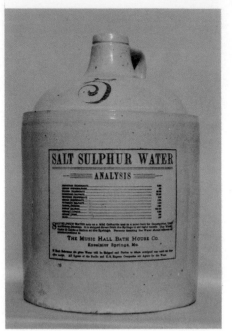

Salt sulphur water from Excelsior Springs, Missouri, was, according to the boast on this jug, "a sure cure for constipation, liver and kidney diseases." The jugs were shipped through the mail with remittance allowed ten days after receipt if "bank references are given." The stamp maker must have had heart failure when commissioned to make this logo. 5 gal. $300.00-350.00.

Not content with mere words, some businesses chose more eye-catching advertsing logos that included pictures as well. Indian likenesses have a special appeal to many collectors. L.-R. 1. 5 gal. $175.00-225.00; 2. 1 gal. (unsigned) $200.00-250.00; 3. 2 gal. (unsigned) $200.00-250.00; 4. 3 gal. $250.00-300.00.

Chicago's many wine and liquor merchants took advantage of this low-cost method of advertising throughout the entire span of Red Wing jug production (1880's-1930's). These three jugs are similar in product advertised (liquor) and in advertising styles (rectangular). Variety and availability make signed advertising jugs such as these excellent buys now and good investments for the future. All ½ gal. L.-R. 1. (RW 11); 2. (M 9); 3. (M 9) $125.00-175.00 ea.

The jugs shown here represent three different jug styles (dome, funnel and shoulder); yet all display attractive oval advertising. L.- R. 1. 2 gal. (M 4) $150.00-200.00; 2. ½ gal. (RW 11) $125.00-175.00; 3. 1 gal. (M 2) $125.00-175.00; 4. ½ gal. (M 5) $125.00-175.00.

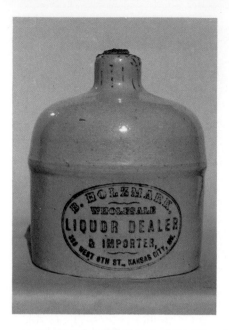

"Decorative doodles" were used in advertising logos to enhance their attractiveness which they obviously did. Also, the unique decorations can be used to identify unmarked pieces of advertising ware as is the case on the two jugs below. The jug on the left is unsigned, though its logo style and decoration is identical to its signed counterpart on the right. All ½ gal. Top L. (RW 6) $200.00-250.00; R (RW 6) $200.00-250.00; Bottom L. (unsigned) $200.00-250.00; R. (RW 11) $250.00-300.00.

Although the shape of the above jug is not unusual, the "banner" style of advertising is. This South Dakota liquor merchant was creative in designing his own logo — another form of "special ordering." ½ gal. (RW 11) $300.00-350.00.

Everything from toilet cleaner to "Dr. Bopp's Hamburger Stomach Bitters" was sold in Red Wing jugs! This St. Paul distiller was the sole U.S. agent for these bitters no less. The premium price for this jug is caused by its equal appeal to bottle collectors. 2 gal. (M 12) $500.00-600.00.

Talk about exclusive advertising! Evidently no request was too difficult. The two Czech merchants for the bottle on the left and the jug below wanted to make sure that their customers could read the logos. This "Bohemian Rye" bottle came from South Dakota. The attached handle is on the opposite side. Signed examples of these bottles are extremely rare. (M 8) $500.00-600.00.

Translation of this Chicago merchant's advertising boasts "The biggest store-house of California wines and liquors." ½ gal. (unsigned). $150.00-175.00.

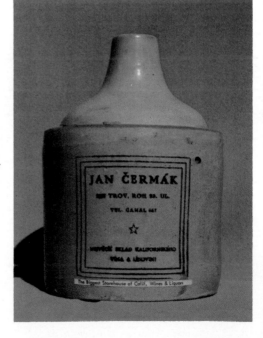

For a whiskey bottle made of glass to be illustrated on this ½ gallon jug is ironic due to the fact that glass would eventually replace stoneware as practical containers. ½ gal. (RW 11) $300.00-350.00.

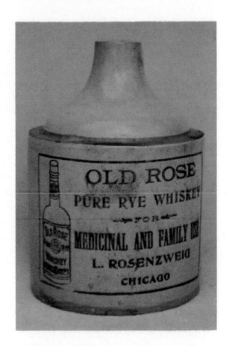

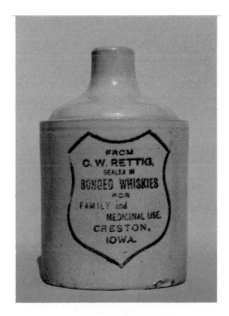

"For Family and Medicinal Use" provided the necessary rationalization, perhaps, for an otherwise teetotaling upstanding member of the community to enjoy a taste of liquor now and then. Both the attractive logos and the small size of these jugs (1 qt.) make thjem desirable additions to any advertising collection. L. (RW 7) R. (M 8) $400.00-450.00 ea.

For collectors living "south of the border," jugs made for merchants in Canada have proven difficult to find. The size of the Imperial gallon shown on the left is, of course, larger than the standard U. S. gallon on the right (both unsigned.) L. $200.00-250.00; R. $150.00-200.00.

A Red Wing Liquor Co. shoulder jug (in the ½ gallon size) is compared here with an Imperial ½ gallon jug made, again, for the Canadian trade. One can't help but wonder what kind of place "Pincher Creek, Alberta" was in the early 1900's. L. $300.00-350.00; R. $250.00-300.00.

Many are the jugs with "liquor" advertising but few are found promoting a "saloon." Not only the simple "Sam's Saloon" logo but also the small 1 quart size make this jug desirable. 1 qt. (unsigned). $400.00-500.00.

Liquor jugs advertising businesses in Red Wing are doubly appealing to Red Wing collectors. Each of the three jugs shown here promotes a different Red Wing company. Brown topped shoulder jugs with advertising were not bottom signed, but the local advertising plus, again, recognizable decorative doodles leave no question as to where these were manufactured. L.-R. All ½ gal. 1. $350.00-400.00; 2. (M 12) $350.00-400.00; 3. $300.00-350.00.

This 1 gallon jug was made to commemorate a holiday excursion via the Mississippi River from Red Wing to St. Paul for potters, their families and guests. Few of these have survived. Due to their scarcity and their connection to the stoneware company itself, they command very high prices when, and if, offered for sale. $1,700.00-2,000.00.

Not only did this successful businessman have five different stores — but he had them in four different states! Collectors from South Dakota, Minnesota, Nebraska and Iowa can all lay claim to this outstanding jug. 2 gal. $300.00-350.00.

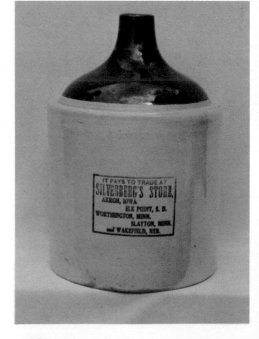

The oval advertisement on the front of this 2 gallon jug measures a full 8" across. This must have been **some** tonic — even then it cost $5 per jug or 6 jugs for $25. The directions on the reverse side are down right comical. Not only are they confusing, but the grammar is appalling. The tonic was a remedy for "well hogs," hogs that "are not doing well" and/or "sick" hogs. Not only have pottery shards of jugs displaying this advertising been found in the dump, but pieces of the stamp used in decorating it have been found as well. $600.00-700.00.

For paper label advertising to have survived in any form through years of hard use is proof of its rarity. This 1 gallon jug is especially nice because it has both paper and stamped advertising. 1 gal. $125.00-150.00.

This later line 5 gallon Red Wing Potteries jug exhibits yet another logo style, an octagon, in keeping with the trademark of the product advertised. The California location contributes to its uniqueness. $225.00-275.00.

Many collectors enjoy assembling "sets" of jugs all displaying the same advertising. John Baum was a Leavenworth, Kansas, liquor dealer who had to move his operation across the Missouri River to Stillings, Missouri, when Kansas went "dry" before prohibition. ½–2 gal. $125.00-150.00 ea.

The odds are against finding three sizes of jugs, each displaying paper advertising from the same vinegar company. Begun in 1881, this business still operates in Chaska, Minnesota, today. L.-R. 1. 1 gal. $60.00-80.00; 2. ½ gal. $60.00-80.00; 3. 1 qt. $125.00-150.00.

Red Wing jugs were used for a lot of things, but as evidence in a court of law? Just such a jug is shown here with a yellowed, brittle paper pasted to it for proof that was to be used later in a lawsuit. On April 4, 1899, the purchaser of this jug filled with whiskey also bought from the same merchant some bitters, supposedly made by the Hostetter Co., which turned out to be "bogus" bitters. The maligned bitters company brought suit against the whiskey company and used this jug as evidence. It is not known who won. ½ gal. (RW 8) $450.00-500.00.

Fancy jugs with their contrasting brown and white glazes were ideally suited for advertising purposes. This 1 gallon example is unique due to its Montana advertising. It was not profitable for the Red Wing stoneware companies to send salesmen so far from Minnesota due to the small population of the western states. Consequently, they appear only infrequently. 1 gal. (RW 8) $350.00-400.00.

These 2 gallon jugs advertise the same company in Atchison, Kansas, and say exactly the same thing but with different logos. The blue diamond is very novel indeed. Both 2 gal. L. (M4); R. (RW 8) $350.00-400.00 ea.

There is very little that could make any of these jugs more attractive. They each display beautiful blue bands, unique and prominent advertising and, best of all, they are all bottom marked. Top, 1 qt. (M 8) $600.00-650.00; Bottom, both 1 gal. (M 9) $650.00-750.00 ea.

Both bottom signed, these bailed jugs are extremely rare. L.-R. 1. (RW 10) $375.00-425.00; 2. (M 12) $1,500.00-1,700.00.

The red printing on this 1 gallon old style long-necked bailed jug makes it unbelievably scarce. The same company continued using the attractive shield logo years later on the 1 gallon Red Wing Union bailed jug — only this time they were selling catsup. L. 1 gal. (RW 6) $400.00-500.00; R. (RWU 1) $250.00-300.00.

This stunning collection showing a variety of bailed jug shapes and sizes all display a "half moon" style of advertising unique to this particular company. L.-R. 1. ½ gal. (RW 6) $200.00-250.00; 2. 1 gal. (RWU 1) $200.00-250.00; 3. 1 qt. (RW 10) $250.00-300.00.; 4. 1 gal. (M 12) $200.00-250.00; 5. ½ gal. (M 12) $200.00-250.00.

Attractive blue printing and a unique bottom marking adorn this bailed jug — the only one shown that actually earns its nickname, "vinegar jug." 1 gal. (M 6) $250.00-300.00.

Pictures of animals add value to any antique — whether it be a wooden butter mold with a carved swan or eagle design or a stoneware pitcher displaying a deer or cow in molded relief. The bear adorning this "Ohio Maple Sap" paper label, therefore, adds charm to an otherwise plain white bailed jug. 1 gal. (RW 7) $150.00-200.00.

Another example of rare picture advertising is used here on a 1 gallon bailed jug. 1 gal. (RW 7) $250.00-300.00.

Crocks

Pictured here is another fine and rare example of salt glaze advertising. The large size of this piece indicates that no item, apparently, was too large to receive advertising treatment. 15 gal. (RW 1) $1,200.00-1,400.00.

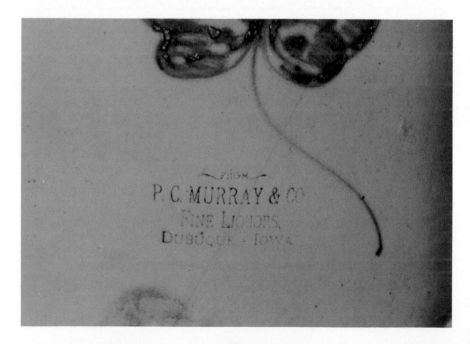

No finer examples of stenciled advertising can be found than on these two salt glazed, hand turned, hand decorated crocks. The word "Crockery" adds to their appeal. Because stenciled advertising was too time consuming to apply, few pieces were labeled in this manner and even fewer examples remain today. Top, (M 2) $1,000.00-1,200.00; Bottom, (unsigned) $1,000.00-1,200.00.

Since L. M. Peirron was a major distributor of Red Wing products in Chicago, he needed something "special" with which to advertise. This window display piece is about as "special" as they come! The red, blue and black printing is all under the glaze. $4,000.00-5,000.00.

This 20 gallon crock has got to be one of the largest pieces ever used for advertising purposes. It obviously wasn't meant to be a "give away." $300.00-350.00.

44

One never tires of reading the logos used to advertise particular businesses. For example, at this "Daylight Cash Store, You Always Get A 'Square Deal'" on "Good Things To Eat and Wear." Are you convinced? $500.00-600.00.

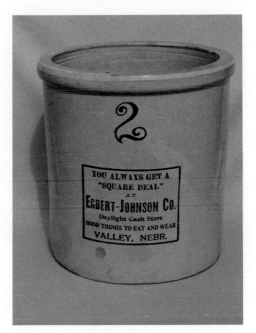

Even more neat Nebraska advertising crocks are shown here. The script style of advertising on the 2 gallon crock on the left is most unusual — probably designed specifically for this merchant or, perhaps, by the merchant himself. (Both unsigned.) $500.00-600.00 ea.

"We Originate, Others Try to Imitate" is a boastful slogan that could have applied to the Red Wing Union Stoneware Co. as well when this crock was made around 1910. Meadow Grove, Nebraska still exists, but it is so small that its population is not given in a current atlas. (unsigned) $500.00-600.00.

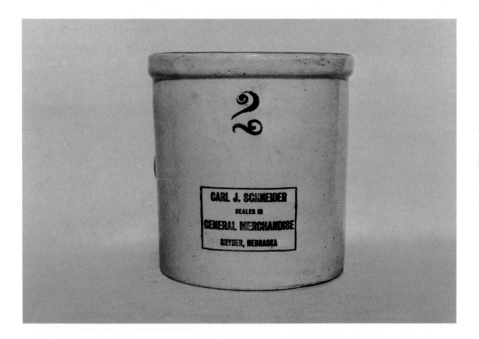

Another 2 gallon "General Merchandise" advertising crock is illustrated here — again, from a VERY small town located in eastern Nebraska. The fact that the merchant's name was "Schneider" and he was located in "Snyder" makes this crock all the more attractive. (unsigned) $500.00-600.00.

The slogan on this Minnesota advertising crock makes one wonder who created some of these innovative colloquial sayings — the merchant or the maufacturer. "Where I was Bought You can get the Most and Best Merchandise for Your Money" won't win any grammatical awards, but it certainly gets the point across. $500.00-600.00.

Not only are the "decorative doodles" distinctive on these two crocks, but the fact that they're from Missouri makes them unique. Ellis and Meadows prided themselves on being "The Farmer's Headquarters" in this northwest Missouri town. $500.00-600.00 ea.

Did this "General Merchandise" merchant from Nebraska give this large gallonage crock away as a premium or did he use it as a container in his store from which merchandise was sold? Either way, we're fortunate that it survived. $700.00-800.00.

Both sides of another fine Nebraska advertising crock are shown here — an exceptional example to say the least. $600.00-700.00.

The large "elephant ear" leaves, the blue printing and the fancy South Dakota advertising oval all contribute to the beauty of this piece. $700.00-800.00.

Another imaginative logo, "The Long Store with the Short Prices," adorns this rare crock — rare not only because it's from Idaho, but also because of the large red wing which is so prominently displayed. $600.00-700.00.

The extra large rims on these 1 gallon crocks help to create deep "tie rings" which allow cloth covers to be held in place by string or twine. L. (M 5) $200.00-250.00; R. (unsigned) $150.00-200.00.

Lucky is the owner of this 1 gallon crock which advertises, of all things, "Red Wing Stoneware" plus "Cigars, Tobacco, Queensware, Dry Goods, Groceries, Hats, Caps, Boots and Shoes, Poultry and Produce." Talk about **general** merchandise! (unsigned) $500.00-600.00.

The small jar shown here is unusual not only for its advertising but also because of its extreme heaviness. Prices, evidently, didn't fluctuate weekly when this item was made. ½ gal. (RW 11) $175.00-225.00; (unsigned) $100.00-150.00.

Crock containers were used by a multitude of businesses as illustrated here. The crocks on the left and the right are both 1 gallon in size, but notice the variation in size. Again, the tie rings for cloth covers are very pronounced. L-R. 1. 1 gal. (RW 7) $200.00-250.00; 2½ gal. (unsigned) $300.00-350.00; 3. 1 gal. (unsigned) $200.00-250.00.

Churns

As rare as salt glazed jugs and crocks with advertising are, this 5 gallon beauty is the only salt glazed churn known to have been given advertising treatment. Although "table relish" seems a strange product ot promote on a butter churn, this company used them almost exclusively. 5 gal. (unsigned) $1,200.00-1,500.00.

Another churn oddity is shown here advertising the same company. It is **one** gallon in size which wasn't even advertised in old Red Wing catalogs. Its identifiable shape, however, and the logo style confirm its maker. The original lid for this churn is a 5¾" white "snuff" jar lid — only with the "button" knob cut out for the dasher. 1 gal. (unsigned) $700.00-900.00.

An additional example of a "Mennig & Slater" advertising churn is pictured here — again with a smaller oval to fit the available space. This one is particularly nice since it also displays the familiar birch leaf motif. 2 gal. $700.00-900.00.

It seems strange that even though the logos are done in black on all three of the churns shown on this page, the gallonage numbers and birch leaves are all blue — an interesting contrast. $800.00-1,000.00 ea.

The red wing and the enormous oval combine to create a very striking and desirable piece of stoneware. 5 gal. $800.00-1,000.00.

Believe it or not, this is one of only three North Dakota advertising pieces in the whole book — strange since the state borders Minnesota. Again, its sparse population probably did not warrant a concentrated sales effort on the part of Red Wing stoneware companies. 6 gal. $800.00-1,000.00.

Because of their size and shape, churns in the 2 gallon size are attractive, no matter what the decoration. This one with advertising, again from Nebraska, implores customers to "Make our Store your Headquarters." 2 gal. $700.00-900.00 (with original lid).

The Ewing, Nebraska, business promoted on this advertising churn boasted of its "Dry-Goods, Clothing, Shoes and Groceries." 4 gal. $800.00-1,000.00.

Water Coolers

Careful examination of this salt glaze water cooler reveals stenciled advertising under the decorated cobalt leaf and glazing. "Twin Springs Water" either welched on its contract or too many such coolers had already been made. (unsigned) $800.00-1,000.00.

Each of these three large water coolers has a different advertising logo. The 6 gallon on the left promotes the Albert Pick Co. (hotels) and the 8 and 10 gallon coolers each display "Book and Stationery Co." advertising (8 gallon — Eau Claire, Wisconsin, and 10 gallon — St. Paul, Minnesota). $500.00-600.00 ea. (with original lids.)

This 3 gallon "cutie" is unique not only because of the "Sunbeam Tea, Russian blend" advertising but also because of the New York location given. $700.00-800.00, complete.

The "Sanitary School Appliances" advertising on this old style cooler reflects their popularity for use in school houses. 8 gal. $600.00-700.00.

Just because this looks like a water cooler without a spigot doesn't mean that it is. In fact, the inside is funnel shaped so that the soda water (in this case) could be "self drained" from the bole in the bottom — thus the name, "self draining jar." The California advertising is unusual as well. 5 gal. $250.00-300.00.

An earlier style of "self draining jar" is shown here. It would have had to sit in a metal ring apparatus of some sort in order for the contents to drain freely. 5 gal. $150.00-200.00.

Miscellaneous Advertising Ware

Even farm products such as chickens and feed needed advertisement. Poultry drinking founts which needed daily attention served this function well. For a "Eureka" feeder such as this to display advertising is rare indeed. (unsigned) $250.00-300.00.

The opposite side of this "bell" style feeder displays the familiar "Red Wing Poultry Drinking Fount" emblem as well as the hand-cut drain opening. This attractive blue circle logo "dresses up" a very utilitarian item. 1 gal. $75.00-100.00 (no base).

Shown here are all four sizes of Red Wing "bell" feeders. Bottom plates are often missing due to the fact that they were used outside and susceptible to the elements. L.-R. 1. 2 gal. $75.00-100.00; 2. 1 qt. $150.00-200.00; 3. 1 gal. $60.00-80.00 (no advertsing); 4. ½ gal. $75.00-100.00 (no bases).

Not only is the feeder on the left desirable due to its size (1 quart), but also because it has the original plate. No matter that the advertising is for a "Seed and Floral Co." L.-R. 1. 1 qt. $200.00-250.00; 2. ½ gal. $100.00-150.00 (complete).

It's strange that "cream" is included with poultry products in this Kansas advertising logo. "Ko-Rec" style feeders with advertising are not easy to find — with or without their original bases. 1 gal. $100.00-150.00 (complete)

The plate for this 3 gallon bottom signed Red Wing Potteries feeder must be enormous. One would also need to have quite a few chickens in order for this piece to be practical. $200.00-250.00.

Two more examples of unique paper label advertising are shown here on signed 10 pound (1 gallon) snuff jars. Both tabacco companies were from Chicago and both have the words "Kaszubska Tabaka" printed below their brand of snuff — strange since the remainder of the advertising is printed in English. Both 1 gal. and (RW8), $100.00-125.00 ea.

One of the nice things about paper labels is that once in a while you can get lucky and find a date. In this case, the tobacco stamp is date 1902. The lid for this 2 pound snuff jar should have an "2" incised in the button handle. 2 lb. (1 qt.) (M8) $125.00-150.00.

Of all things on which to advertise your business! This spitton certainly was not used as a container for merchandise nor was it likely to have been given away as a premium. Maybe the merchant just wanted to show off the latest thing for use in public places. (unsigned) $500.00-600.00.

These vases were premiums given away by various florists. The two below display two different logos used by a Kansas City floral company. Old Red Wing catalogs verify the authenticity of their maker. The beauty of each is enhanced by the blue advertising. $400.00-500.00 ea.

Product Lines: Kitchen Advertising Ware

After 1920 kitchen items were, by far, the most common lines to display advertising and to be used as "give aways." It makes sense, since they were pieces that a housewife most often used. They still add decorative touches to kitchens today. The variety of slogans and logo styles displayed add a special charm.

The Red Wing Union Stoneware Co. in promotional literature sent to merchants not only suggested slogans from which merchants could choose (albeit some were pretty "corny"), but they also came out with a whole new kitchen line on which advertising could be prominently displayed. They called it "gray line;" collectors today commonly refer to it as "spongeband." Can't you just imagine a reamer or cake stand emblazoned with some merchant's sales pitch? It's possible!

"Pay cash, It pays" and "It pays to mix with ..." serve as reminders in the advertisements shown on these spongeband pieces. One tantalizing testimonial used by the stoneware company in its literature was: "One merchant had his name and telephone number stamped on the inside bottom of a casserole. Eight hundred of them went like hot cakes at 30¢ a piece ... and every clerk in the store that evening was boasting about his sales record." Oh, if we could only have been at that store that day! Bowl, $150.00-200.00; Small pitcher, $300.00-350.00; Casserole, $275.00-325.00 (with lid).

Dating product lines is much easier if the businessman had the year included in the ad he selected for his promotional "give away." Two beautiful examples of dated advertising are displayed here on a spongeband pitcher and, lo and behold, a hanging salt jar. Pitcher, $350.00-400.00 if dated; $275.00-325.00 undated; Hanging salt, $1,000.00-1,200.00 complete.

Beater jars and custard cups were also used for advertising purposes. Another testimonial included in some Red Wing Union Stoneware promotional literature stated that "Another merchant offered a beater jar at cost to everyone who would bring in a case of eggs. You didn't find the farmers in that community shopping around for better prices ... they came in for the JAR!" Top (custard cup) $250.00 300.00; Bottom (beater jar) $275.00-325.00.

Another popular kitchen line that was often used for advertising purposes in the 1930's was the saffron line. Unfortunately, if the pieces were used at all, they very likely show unsightly seepage due to the more porous clay used. If, on the other hand, they retain their original appearance, they are extremely attractive and highly sought after due to the present popularity of yellow ware.

The advertising logos make the saffron pitchers shown above and the beater jar pictured below much prettier than their plain counterparts would be. Pitchers, $175.00-225.00 ea.; Beater jar, $125.00-150.00.

The smallest size casserole in this line (4½" diameter) is nearly impossible to find with or without advertising. $275.00-325.00 (with original lid).

These "cookie jars" must have been used by their owners for other purposes due to the apparent seepage. Nevertheless, the bold black advertising against their yellow background provides an interesting contrast. $75.00-125.00 ea. (with seepage); $125.00-150.00 (mint with lids).

Although many of the same molds were used first for the spongeband line and later the saffron kitchenware (pitchers, hanging salts, casseroles, and beater jars), nappies and pie plates were unique to the saffron line. Red Wing pie plates of any kind are desirable additions to any Red Wing collection. The inside of the pie plate shown below displays the same "Haack's Store" advertising as does the nappie above. Top, $100.00-125.00; Bottom, $175.00-200.00.

Besides the familiar brown and white stripes which adorn most saffron pieces, red and blue sponging was also used occasionally for decorating – particularly on bowls. $75.00-100.00 ea.

Advertising pieces with dates included are all very rare with the exception of the Lampert Yards 1937 Anniversary saffron sponge bowls. The company must have done a booming business, as many of these bowls are known to exist. The date indicates that these bowls were made by Red Wing Potteries. $75.00-100.00 ea.

In addition to the special lines of kitchenware (spongeband and saffron ware) that the Red Wing Union Stoneware Co. designed with advertising in mind, most other kitchen items adapted easily to this venture. The rest of this chapter will be devoted to all kinds of kitchen products used for advertising purposes.

Bowls

Red Wing made several bowls using this same mold, but no others were glazed in this fashion. Blue sponge has a universal appeal. $125.00-150.00.

Not only is this the hardest style to find of any of the "cap" bowls, but this one also comes with advertising. $300.00-350.00.

Three different bowl styles, paneled sponge, blue/white Indian Goodluck, and ridged sponge; again display a variety of slogans and logo styles from which a merchant could choose. $125.00-175.00 ea.

Most blue and all brown stoneware bowls are the same color all over. If advertising was to be used, however, the inside was glazed white. The advertising logo for "Red Wing Flour" makes the bowl above very desirable even though it is unsigned. The white and brown bowls below are much prettier when given advertising treatment. "Buy it from 'Hon' and You'll Save 'Mon'" adds character to the bowl on the bottom right. Top (unsigned) $150.00-200.00; Bottom (unsigned) $65.00-85.00 ea.

This ½ pint bowl is so small that the advertising covers the whole inside bottom. (unsigned) $80.00-100.00.

Red Wing Stoneware Co. produced 7" beater bowls for the Columbia Metal Products Co. by the thousands, though very few of them, like this one, are bottom signed as well. An original Dunlap beater for use with the bowl is also shown. Bowl, (RW 11) $50.00-60.00; (unsigned) $30.00-40.00.

Advertising logos are the only decorations that these all white casseroles (above) and stew pans (below) need in order to achieve a simple beauty. Top (unsigned) $75.00-100.00 ea. (with original lids); Bottom (unsigned) $100.00-125.00.

Pitchers and Mugs

Cherryband pitchers proved to be one of the most popular lines with merchants to be used for advertising purposes. Notice the creativity involved in designing both the logo shapes and styles and the slogans themselves. Prices depend on color, sharpness of mold, and the advertising itself. All of the ones shown on this page are medium in height. Top, L.-R. 1. $200.00-250.00; 2. $350.00-400.00; 3. $250.00-300.00; Bottom, $250.00-300.00.

The good color, sharp mold markings, and bold, attractive logo all add value to this pitcher. $300.00-350.00.

Represented here are all three sizes of the popular cherryband pitcher and three styles of advertising — oval, circle, and rectangle. The largest and smallest pitchers in this pattern are the most difficult to find. L.-R. 1. $400.00-500.00; 2. $200.00-250.00; 3. $600.00-700.00.

This cherryband pitcher is another special-order piece because of its rare all white glaze. Its uniqueness is extended even further due to the picture advertising and the date given (1914). August Becker was a local Red Wing grocer who also had ties to the Red Wing Union Stoneware Co. $800.00-1,000.00.

As rare as the all white "Becker" pitcher is, this blue and white example seems to be one of a kind. Becker obviously wanted his premiums to be different from all other cherryband pitchers. 1914 is the earliest date known on any cherryband advertising logo and is thought to indicate the beginning of blue/white glaze production. Note how sharp and detailed the mold markings are on both of these examples — proof that they were among the first out of the mold. $1,500.00-2,000.00.

Though relatively common in a blue/white glaze, this cherryband patterned pitcher qualifies as a special order item due to its all-over sponge design. The Peterson Co. was located in Winona, Minnesota, and was a good Red Wing customer as many other kitchen stoneware pieces can be found with their logo. $800.00-1,000.00.

This entirely new pitcher shape was created for advertising purposes. It has been found most often with a "Hull, Ia." firm advertised on the inside bottom, but one has been found with "Elliot, N.D." advertising as well. Whoever came up with the idea for its design was extremely ingenious. $700.00-800.00.

As was the case with the "cherryband" pitcher for merchants Becker and Peterson, this "iris" patterned pitcher got special treatment for this particular Iowa businessman, a veterinarian no less. Iris pitchers are more commonly found with a single colored glaze — blue, brown, "mulberry," cream, etc., but this sponge example is truly stunning. (RWP 1) $1,200.00-1,500.00.

Although one wouldn't normally look at the bottom of a pitcher while using it, this Wisconsin merchant chose that location for his logo on this barrel pitcher. The example on the right has no advertising, but it is signed "Made in Red Wing" on the bottom which proves the authenticity of the one on the left. $125.00-175.00.

The bottoms of mugs, on the other hand, would be seen (by someone else, of course) every time the user would take a drink. So, in addition to the raised "G" and the star shown on the white mug's front, "The Gluek Brewing Co." (Minneapolis 1894–1957) is stamped in blue on the bottom. $110.00-135.00 ea.

Likewise, another beverage company chose this "Happy Days Are Here Again" mug bottom on which to display its message. The ending of prohibition (1933) was an occasion to be celebrated. $75.00-100.00.

The unusual logos shown on these mugs required more ingenuity than did the simple geometric designs displayed on many advertising pieces. L.-R. 1. $200.00-250.00; 2. $175.00-225.00; 3. $150.00-200.00.

The dates on the mug above and the middle one below (1909 and 1933) indicate their prolonged popularity. The mug on the right below is the only one shown with the logo placement on the side rather than the front. Its message implores the user to "Have One on the B. & D. Hardware." $150.00-200.00.

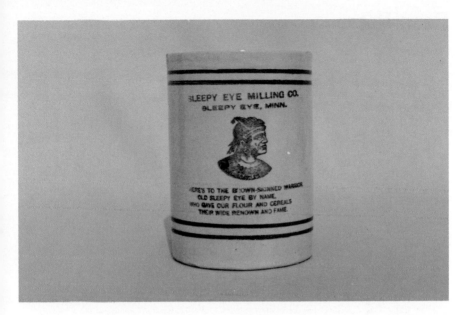

These Sleepy Eye mugs or "steins" were made by the Minnesota Stoneware Co. shortly after the turn of the century, presumably to be given as premiums in the flour sacks of the Sleepy Eye Minn. Milling Co. The "verse" mug on the top is also bottom signed. Chief Sleepy Eye's likeness on the bottom is much larger, leaving no room for the "verse" and, also, it has no bottom mark. $1,500.00-1,800.00 ea.

These mugs have appeal not only to collectors of Red Wing stoneware but also to collectors of Old Sleepy Eye memorabilia — thus, one reason for their high value.

Bean Pots

This all white bailed bean pot could very well be a special order piece made especially for F.W. Dahl. Advertising turns a common brown and white example on the left into an uncommon collectible. $125.00-150.00 ea.

Though seldom signed, Red Wing made this newer style bean pot by the thousands. They were among the most popular of all product lines to be used for advertising. $65.00-85.00.

This particular advertisement is interesting because of the type of business advertised — that of "Advertising Specialities." $65.00-85.00.

Plain brown, bottom signed, custard cups, or "individual bean pots," are not all that uncommon, but for one to be all white with advertising as well is quite extraordinary. (RW 12) $150.00-200.00.

Butter Crocks

The myriad of dairies and creameries in the upper midwest (the heart of Red Wing's marketing area) provided a widespread market for advertising butter crocks in the early 1900's. Due to their prevalent use then, many fine examples can be found today. They are, therefore, likely candidates for good investments in the future, since they are still reasonably priced. How can one be sure that an unsigned butter crock is of Red Wing origin since most were not marked with the company maker? Studying the logo style; comparing the "decorative doodle" used (if any) with other signed Red Wing pieces using the same adornment; and lots of "hands on" experience checking glaze, clay, mold design, and "feel" is the best advice.

Instructions such as "Return to," "Take Me Back," and "Property of" indicate that butter jars were to be reused each time another purchase of butter was made. Disposable packaging was unknown in those days — as were health and sanitation requirements. Not only dairy products but also "baked beans," "pastry," and "tea" were examples of other products featured on this medium. All of the logos displayed on these jars are in the striking and, consequently, more desirable blue printing. $200.00-250.00 (bottom signed); $125.00-175.00 (unsigned).

The one thing that these particular butter crocks have in common is that they are **all** bottom signed. Otherwise they represent four different sizes (2, 3, 5, and 10 pounds) and exhibit three charming "decorative doodles." L.-R. 1. (RW 8) $200.00-250.00; 2. (RW 7) $200.00-250.00; 3. (RWU 1) $200.00-250.00; 4. (M 12) $300.00-350.00.

The bottom markings on these two butter crocks indicate that they were made before 1906. The merchant who advertised on the right crock was so confident of his fame, evidently, that he didn't even bother with the town or state. L. 10 lb. (M12) $200.00-225.00; R. 3 lb. (M 12) $200.00-225.00.

What are the odds of two different creamery companies in two different states having the same name? Both logos include a "crescent" moon and star motif though they are distinctively unique. The St. Paul butter crock has, in addition, a rare double Minnesota bottom marking which adds greatly to its value. Top, 2 lb. (M 6) $350.00-400.00; Bottom, 2 lb. (unsigned) $125.00-175.00.

Wouldn't it be wonderful (then **and** now) to get a glimpse inside a store that makes the claim "We Sell Everything?" Red Wing items with North Dakota advertising are extremely rare, yet here are two butter crocks each advertising different general merchandise stores in the same small town! (unsigned) $125.00-175.00.

Again, the blue advertising and the fancy decoration turn a mundane white butter crock into a work of art. Stieren and Jerman must have had a prosperous general merchandise business in West Point, Nebraska, because this same oval advertising logo also appears on two beehive jugs, a ½ gallon shoulder jug, a 3 gallon crock, a 6 gallon churn and a ½ gallon crock in other sections of this book. 2 lb. (RW 8) $300.00-350.00.

This merchant didn't want any customer to miss the message, so he had printing stamped on opposite sides of this small butter crock ... but ice cream and **bread**? 2 lb. (unsigned) $200.00-250.00.

Though unsigned, there's little doubt as to the manufacturer of these butter crocks since Red Wing is located in Goodhue County. $200.00-250.00 ea.

The logos on these Chicago butter crocks all look the same, but close examination reveals that the addresses are different. Kuhlman had two stores on Lake Street in Chicago. For a 3 gallon crock to advertise "Butter" is unusual. L.-R. 10 lb., 1 gal. & 3 lb. (all unsigned) $125.00-175.00 each; 3 gal. $400.00-500.00.

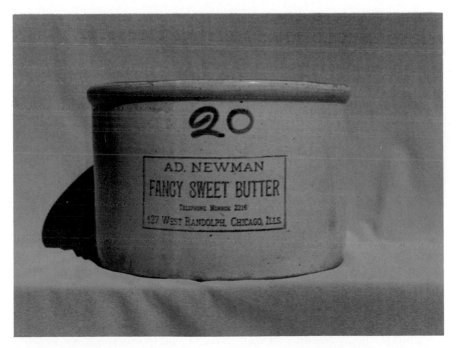

The hand drawn "20" on this large butter crock indicates that it was an early white glaze production piece. Large butter crocks are very seldom seen with advertising. (unsigned) $350.00-400.00.

Another 20 pound butter crock, again exhibiting Chicago advertising, makes one wonder about the difference in taste between "fancy sweet and salt butter." The blue bands certainly add a decorative touch. (unsigned) $400.00-500.00.

Cottage cheese was another dairy product sold in crocks similar to those containing butter. This 10 pound example, like the "Hruska" one above, is especially desirable due to its resemblance to the highly prized Red Wing pantry jars. (unsigned) $400.00-500.00.

94

With or without advertising, pantry jars are among the most desirable items for Red Wing collectors today. 5 lb. $500.00-600.00 (with original lid).

Advertising displayed on this size of pantry jar (1 pound) is infreqently found. The novel slogan adds to its attractiveness. $550.00-600.00 (with original lid).

Similar in design to regular pantry jars, the single top and bottom blue bands, unique lid, and differing size make this "Pitts Bros." jar a special-order item. $500.00-600.00 (with original lid).

Refrigerator Jars and Bailed Jars

Stacking refrigerator jars were ideally shaped for circular advertising logos. The two with advertising shown here are both medium sized. $200.00-250.00 ea.

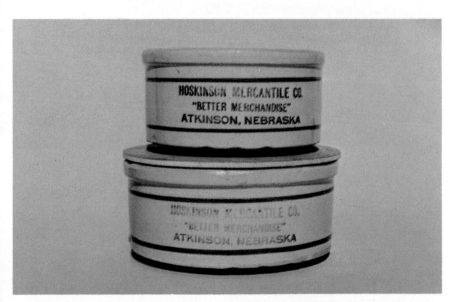

These two Atkinson, Nebraska, advertising beauties are unusual not only because of the frontal placement of the advertising but also because they are both different sizes — large and medium. $225.00-275.00 ea.

Two different styles of bailed "Refrigerator Jars" are illustrated both in the photo above and the one below. Blue/white ones usually do not have advertising and most white examples with blue bands normally do not say "Red Wing Refrigerator Jar." Thus, each of these is unique. $275.00-325.00 ea. (complete)

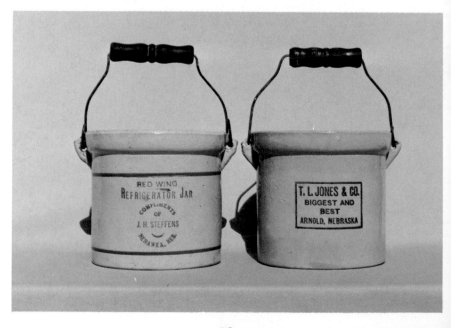

More bailed jars are displayed here — all in the 3 pound size. Though the middle jar contains no advertising, it is included to show what most of them were probably used for. The jar on the right also displays advertising for a Beaver City, Nebraska, store on the opposite side. L.-R. 1. $300.00-350.00; 2. $175.00-225.00; 3. $250.00-300.00 (with original lids).

A Wisconsin merchant liked these jars so much that he had them made in both the 3 and 5 pound sizes. $250.00-300.00 (with original lids).

The Hazel Pure Food Co. was evidently a good customer of the Red Wing Stoneware Co., as numerous bailed jars displaying a variety of advertising styles and a variety of products sold have been found. Though they are all 5 pounds in size, their shape is taller and slimmer than the standard 5 pound refrigerator jar shape — thus qualifying them as having special order status. (signed) (RW 11) $200.00-250.00 ea.; (unsigned) $150.00-200.00.

Beater Jars

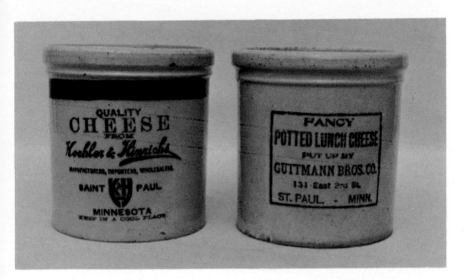

Each of these jars, from different St. Paul companies, advertises the same product. They are ½ gallon in size, have rounded "beater jar" bottoms, and are extremely heavy. Kohler and Hinrichs, however, dressed their container up a bit by including the wide blue band and more innovative printing styles. L.-R. 1. (M 9) $200.00-250.00; 2. (M 12) $150.00-200.00; (unsigned) $100.00-125.00 ea.

Though Western Stoneware also made this style of beater jar, the advertising styles exhibited here plus the "decorative doodle" on the McCool Jct. jar lend credence to the argument that these particular ones are Red Wing products. The "tie ring" around the jar tops also seems to be a Red Wing trait. $125.00-175.00 ea.

Round bottoms in these beater jars made them convenient household necessities. They were artistically suited for advertising due to their size and white glaze as is evidenced here. $125.00-175.00 ea.

The middle example is included not only to show the standard Red Wing logo which appears on the opposite sides of the advertising jars but also to illustrate its atypical use of double blue bands on the top and bottom. $125.00-175.00 ea.

This beater jar is a fine example of an unusual glaze design applied to a common mold piece in order to achieve a stunning appearance. The clover leaf in the logo design adds additional charm. $600.00-700.00.

Canning Jar

This bailed "packing" or canning jar has a lot of things going for it — it is small in size (1 quart), has an attractive "shield" advertising logo, and is bottom signed. (RW 10) $250.00-300.00.

 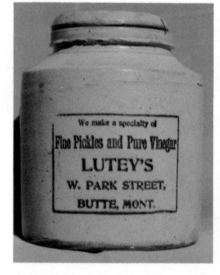

The red glaze on the lids and bottoms of these "safety valve" jars was used to align the two parts for proper sealing. The sealing hardware is next to impossible to find today as are advertising examples of these jars. L. ½ gal. (M 8) $150.00-175.00; R. ½ gal. (RW 11) $250.00-300.00.

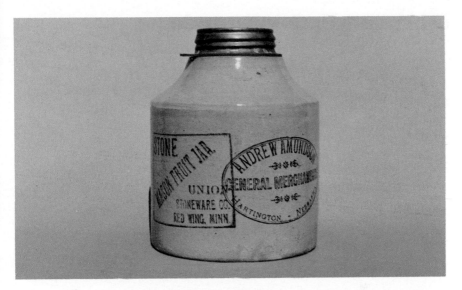

Only two of these ½ gallon canning jars displaying both the "Stone Mason Fruit Jar" logo and Andrew Amundson's creative advertisement for his Hartington, Nebraska, general merchandise business are known. Too bad his establishment wasn't in an urban area like Chicago so that there might be more of these around! $2,000.00-2,500.00.

Though unsigned in any fashion, there is little doubt as to the manufacturer of these two fruit jars. Notice, again, that the "decorative doodle" on the jar to the right is identical to the one used on the Stone Mason jar above. These two once again promote Nebraska merchants. L. 1 qt. $1,000.00-1,500.00; R. ½ gal. $1,500.00-2,000.00.

CHAPTER II: Miniature Jugs

What better way to promote, commemorate and/or celebrate something than to give or sell a cute little miniature jug as a remembrance. Whether it be a company product, convention, state fair, or a football rivalry, the intent was the same — the recipient had a small memento to take home that would serve as a reminder of the product and/or occasion. Of all the products Red Wing made, these are probably among the most sought after by collectors today. Consequently, since the demand far exceeds the present supply, many of these jugs bring huge sums of money when, and if, they are offered for sale.

The city of Red Wing itself took advantage of one of its major industries in order to promote, ostensibly, tourism and the convention trade. Shown here are three typical miniature jug shapes (fancy, cone, and ovoid) plus three different "Souvenir of Red Wing" logo styles. L.-R. 1. (M 10) $400.00-450.00; 2. $300.00-350.00; 3. $450.00-500.00; 4. $300.00-350.00; 5. $325.00-375.00.

A slightly different logo style is represented on these two jugs. Blue printing always seems to add to the beauty and desirability of any piece. L. $425.00-475.00; R. $375.00-425.00.

Two additional Red Wing promotional logos are illustrated here. The greeting on the jug on the left is as warm and inviting to collectors today as it was to convention goers then. The plain black stamp used on the jug on the right seems to have been used very rarely as it appears on only two known items. L. $375.00-425.00; R. (M 10) $450.00-550.00.

The unusual tan bottom color, blue and white bands, and the Minnesota circle stamp all combine to make this small jug not only attractive, but rare as well. Each of these unique additions required extra time in manufacturing which could mean that it was made for a special occasion. $1,000.00-1,200.00.

Not only is the jug on the left the oldest Red Wing mini known (1880's), but it is also the only one that was hand turned as opposed to being molded. It is smaller in size than the ⅛ pint fancy jug on the right which was used to promote a Union Stoneware Co. branch office in Chicago before 1906. L. $800.00-1,000.00; R. $700.00-900.00.

After the Red Wing and Minnesota Stoneware Companies joined in 1906, they became one entity — the Red Wing Union Stoneware Co. These "shoulder" jugs represent two different sizes and three different logo styles. They were used to promote the new "union." L.-R. 1. $600.00-700.00; 2. $650.00-750.00; 3. $600.00-700.00; 4. $400.00-450.00.

Any mini jug that displays an under-the-glaze red wing is extremely desirable, and this particular one is probably the ultimate collector's prize. $1,000.00-1,200.00.

Conventions were, evidently, a staple of the Red Wing economy. The Elks and the Moose Lodge met in the city of Red Wing on succeeding years and chose these unique white and ovoid shaped jugs to commemorate their meetings. L. $400.00-450.00; R. (RWU 3) $400.00-450.00.

The creativity and detail involved in the logo design for this convention commemorative jug is unequaled. Its early 1909 date indicates that, even then, Red Wing was a desirable place to visit. $450.00-500.00.

What **is** known about this jug is that it is very beautiful and rare. What is **not** known is what the initials B.M.I.U. stands for. But then, who cares! Right? ½ pint. $1,000.00-1,200.00.

Three other groups of conventioneers found Red Wing to be an inviting place — the postal workers in 1939, the Southern Minnesota Medical Association in 1915, and the Order of the Redmen in 1927. Creativity in logo design surfaces again on the middle jug, as it is printed in the form of a prescription for the doctors attending. L.-R. 1. $350.00-400.00; 2. $700.00-800.00; 3. $500.00-600.00.

One of the biggest purchasers of mini fancy jugs was Excelsior Springs, Missouri. These were filled with samples of their famous mineral water. Two different logo styles are shown here with the 1903 stamping being the more difficult to find. Each set is shown in the four miniature fancy jug sizes (⅛ pint, ¼ pint, ½ pint, and 1 pint). Top (signed) $275.00-325.00 ea; Pt. (unsigned) $200.00-250.00; other sizes (unsigned) $175.00-200.00; Bottom (signed) $300.00-350.00; (unsigned) $200.00-250.00.

All five of these fancy jugs are ½ pint in size. The advertising represents four different states — Illinois, Montana, Nebraska, and Iowa — proof of their popularity when made and a good reason for it now. Top, (RW 10) $275.00-325.00 ea.; (unsigned) $175.00-225.00 ea.; Bottom, L.-R. 1. (unsigned) $175.00-200.00; 2. (unsigned) $200.00-250.00; 3. (unsigned) $125.00-175.00; if signed $250.00-300.00 ea.

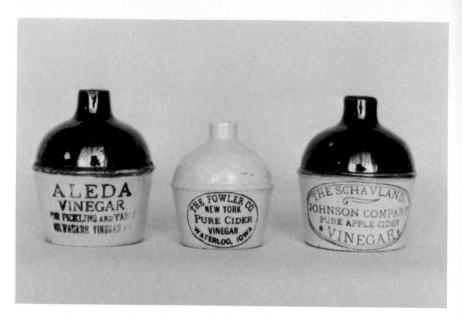

Miniature jugs provided merchants an economical means with which to promote their businesses. Many of them contained samples of the product sold — in this case it was vinegar. These ⅛ and ¼ pint jugs add charm to any collection. The all white one in the middle has not been found with any other advertising. L.-R. 1. ¼ pt. (unsigned) $150.00-175.00; 2. ⅛ pt. (unsigned) $300.00-350.00; 3. ¼ pt. (M 10) $275.00-325.00.

The rare size (1 pint) and bold, simple advertising logo make this jug a delight to behold. Do you suppose that this is the same "Schoch" who advertised on the butter crock on page 89? If so, he again left off the city and state. Where **was** he located, anyway? 1 pt. (unsigned) $225.00-275.00.

Reversing the location of the advertising on this jug was intentional so that a paper label could be applied to the "front." Jahreiss, being a liquor dealer, was proud of the fact that his products were not diluted, which was a common practice in the early 1900's; therefore, he was a "Seller of Pure Goods." His original building still stands at this address in Owatonna. 1 pt. (unsigned) $275.00-325.00.

The small size (⅛ pint) and the bottom markings each contribute to the desirability of these two jugs. Both (M 10) $400.00-500.00 ea.

Bold blue printing adds to the attractiveness of this advertising jug. ½ pt. (unsigned) $175.00-225.00.

Each of the hotels advertised on these jugs (the Nicollet in Minneapolis and the Merchants in St. Paul) were among the oldest and finest in each city. Both were torn down and rebuilt — occasions that were commemorated and celebrated with these miniature ⅛ pint fancies. Notice the variance in shapes and glazes of the two Merchants jugs on the right. All unsigned. L.-R. 1. $275.00-325.00; 2. $325.00-375.00; 3. $325.00-375.00.

The holiday season was a popular time for merchants to show their appreciation to good customers. For this paper label to have survived for over 80 years in such excellent condition is extremely rare. ½ pt. (unsigned) $125.00-175.00.

Men's after shave was sold in these ½ pint fancies by the Bergholt Co. of Minneapolis. The painted logos were done after the glazing, so it is difficult to find them in good condition. The advertising reads "Old Fashioned, Gay 90's, Bergholt's, All American" on one side and "Father, Gay 90's" with a picture of a man's face on the other. $50.00-75.00 ea.

L.M. Pierron operated his own pottery company in Milwaukee until 1893 when he was forced to close due to poor economic conditions and stiff competition. At that time he became a distributor for several other stoneware companies, including the Union Stoneware Co. of Red Wing. This ¼ pint fancy jug was made by Red Wing for Pierron to use as a promotional give away. Any Pierron advertising piece is desirable not only to Red Wing collectors but to Wisconsin pottery enthusiasts as well; thus, they command high prices. (unsigned) $400.00-500.00.

Even miniature jugs could be special ordered. These examples are especially appealing due to the "crockery" advertising, the unique shape, an underglaze red wing, and a pouring spout. This St. Paul company began their operation after 1914. ⅛ pt. $400.00-500.00.

This ⅛ pint cone top miniature jug is another example of an advertising piece unrelated to the business and/or product advertised. Whatever does a little jug have to do with Atwater-Kent radios? $275.00-325.00.

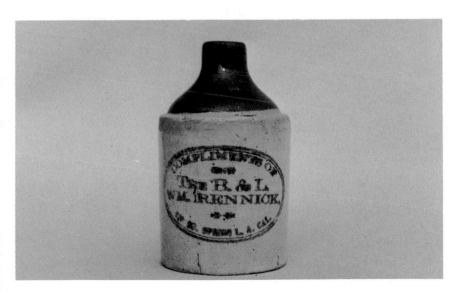

Collectors of Red Wing have just recently begun to realize the amount of Red Wing products that were made to advertise California businesses. It is, as yet, nearly an untouched market. This mini "shoulder" jug from Los Angeles is a prime example. (unsigned) $250.00-300.00.

A five-gallon beehive "little brown jug" has been a symbol of the football rivalry between Minnesota and Michigan since 1909. Many ⅛ pint fancy variations were used over the years to promote the annual event. It was recently learned that in 1930 two University of Minnesota students pooled their resources and ordered 5,000 miniature jugs (minimum order for stenciled pieces) from their local Red Wing office to sell at that year's game. They paid 20¢ each and tried to sell them for 50¢ each. It proved to be a financial disaster and they were still paying off their debt after they graduated. L.-R. 1. $350.00-400.00; 2. $175.00-225.00; 3. $150.00-200.00 (all unsigned)

Because of the large minimum order that Red Wing required for stenciling, it was easier and cheaper to use paper labels or paint on plain jugs or to have a pin made to stick into the cork tops for jugs to be sold at games. L.-R. 1. $75.00-100.00; 2. $100.00-125.00; 3. $50.00-75.00 (all unsigned)

For many years the Red Wing Union Stoneware Co. had a large "booth" advertising their business at the annual Minnesota State Fair. A small kiln was set up so that mini jugs such as these were fired on the spot and given away. L.-R. 1. $275.00-325.00; 2. $300.00-350.00 (both unsigned).

The Red Wing company went through another name change in 1936 (Red Wing Potteries) and once again used mini jugs to help promote a new image. This particular logo was used as a bottom marking on many art pottery vases. ⅛ pt. (unsigned) $425.00-475.00.

These ⅛ pint fancies had no handles so that a cloth or metal seal could go over the cork and be secured with wire or string. The paper labels shown here indicate eastern markets. "Mercury" is stamped on the opposite side of the jug on the right. L.-R. (unsigned) 1. $125.00-150.00; 2. $100.00-125.00; 3. $125.00-150.00.

Other stoneware companies made cone top mercury jugs, but those from Red Wing have a rectangular frame around "Mercury." This particular style of jug came with or without handles and in four sizes ranging from ⅛ pint to 1 pint. L.-R. (unsigned) 1. $75.00-100.00; 2. $75.00-100.00; 3. $100.00-125.00.

A star appears once again on the logo of these mercury containers. Red Wing verification is obvious when compared to the "Souvenir" piece below. The small red wing and the blue printing are truly stunning on the all white background. Only one of these gems is known at this time. Top, $100.00-125.00 ea.; Bottom, $800.00-1,000.00.

Later mini jugs advertising Red Wing pottery were decorated with wing paper labels. Some of these were made as late as the 1940's. Considering that the first dated mini jug known is 1902, they obviously served as a successful medium for promotional purposes. L.-R. 1. and 2. $50.00-75.00; 3. and 4. $50.00-75.00 ea.

Another unique "bottle" shape is represented here on the left and right hand miniatures. They are similar in design to the advertising gin or wine bottle shown at the top of page 28. The middle "Egyptian" jug is more typically found in both brown and white glaze rather than just all brown. (unsigned) $40.00-60.00 ea.

For Red Wing collectors, the surprises never end. These jugs appear to be from the same mold as the jugs shown at the top of page 108 and at the bottom of page 110. They were "discovered" in the Red Wing area and both have "Feb. 21, 1909" written in pencil on their bottoms. Chief Red Wing's name before becoming chief was "Walking Buffalo." Could this be the tie-in? At any rate, they remain a beautiful mystery. (both unsigned) L. $500.00-600.00; R. $300.00-400.00.

"Beauty" needs a new definition when it's used to describe these blue sponged jugs. They are simply gorgeous. What's even more unbelieveable is that the ½ pint on the left is bottom signed! L. ½ pt. (RW 10) $2,000.00-2,500.00; R. ¼ pt. (unsigned) $1,200.00-1,500.00.

CHAPTER III:
Miscellaneous Stoneware Collectibles

In addition to jugs in minature form, the Red Wing companies made scaled down models of other objects — including everything from shoes to animals to sewer pipes. Some of these items were intended for promotional purposes, others for practical use, and still others were made as toys for children. One product subject which was commonly manufactured in miniature form by many stoneware companies was a canteen or flask.

Any Red Wing stoneware canteen is a hard-to-find item. Both of these probably date between the years 1900 and 1908. The canteen on the right is an extremely rare find. There are no other markings on either piece. $450.00-550.00 ea.

Another heretofore unknown California item is this nifty San Francisco miniature advertising canteen. Gustav H. Erb was most likely a liquor dealer or a tavern owner. (unsigned) $250.00-300.00.

Above and below are front and back views of two small canteens. On the left in both photos is an early whiteware example and on the right, an outstanding example of an even earlier salt glaze canteen. Both items were made for L.M. Pierron, a distributor for Red Wing in Milwaukee, Wisconsin. From time to time he would commission Red Wing to make items with his company's name. It is assumed, therefore, that these pieces were manufactured in Red Wing since they have all the Red Wing characteristics. L. $350.00-400.00; R. $450.00-550.00.

The shoe industry was (and still is) a major factor contributing to the city of Red Wing's healthy economy. What better reason, therefore, to choose that subject for a miniature stoneware piece. Acquiring these specialty items could make an interesting challenge for any collector — particularly outside of the Red Wing area. Careful examination of the seam stitching between the heel and side of some of these shoes indicates, faintly, the words "Minn. S.W. Co." The attractive deep blue shoe on the right is among the most desirable. Additional colors, not pictured here, are bisque (unglazed), yellow, and light brown. (signed) Depending on color, $250.00-300.00 ea.; (unsigned) $125.00-150.00.

"Toy" miniature spittoons were listed on an 1896 price list and sold for 10¢ each. What on earth did children do with them? These two examples show some variation in shape, but each is approximately 2" tall. $300.00-350.00 ea.

Two different styles of traveling bags testify to the diversity of miniatures produced by the stoneware companies. The bag on the the the left was produced for the 1912 United Commercial Travelers' Convention and is a tiny bottle. The bottoms of both are displayed below. $450.00-500.00 ea.

Although John H. Rich was president of the Red Wing Stoneware Co., he allowed others to run the business in 1892 so that he could devote his attention and energy to the sewer pipe end of the business. In 1893, the John H. Rich Sewer Pipe Works was formally established and even shared its office for a while with the Red Wing Stoneware Co. $225.00-250.00.

This beautifully salt glazed sewer pipe sample had to have been made between 1896 (when the John H. Rich Sewer Pipe Works and the Red Wing Sewer Pipe Co. joined to form the Union Sewer Pipe Co.) and 1901 when they changed their name to the Red Wing Sewer Pipe Co. $225.00-250.00.

To advertise the very profitable sewer pipe enterprise, many sewer pipe samples were made and given away. The piece above is the back view of the middle sample below. It extols the virues of the clay used. It, plus the example shown on the bottom left, were made from actual sewer pipe clay. The piece on the right, however, is made from pottery and is more commonly found. The sewer pipe industry continued in Red Wing until the 1970's. Top, $125.00-150.00; Bottom, far left, $45.00-60.00; far right (pottery) $35.00-45.00.

Front and back views of a badger on a football (above) and a gopher on a tree stump (below) are shown here. The stump serves as a toothpick holder. Although not pictured, there is also a gopher on a football. The football miniatures were sold as souvenirs of the football rivalry between the Universities of Minnesota and Wisconsin. Footballs, $100.00-125.00; Stumps, $125.00-150.00.

Animals

Animals produced by Red Wing were successful sellers even though they served no utilitarian purpose except, perhaps, as toys. In an 1895 price list, pigs sold for 12½¢ each, dogs for 18¢, and cows and calves for 40¢.

The traditional color found on most bulldogs is chestnut brown, above, but the striking bulldog below received very special treatment as affirmed by the uncommon black glaze, white chest and paw tips, and painted eyes and mouth. Top, $475.00-550.00; Bottom, $550.00-650.00.

The large, almost jet-black pig measures 7" long while the small one is 5" long. What better choice to represent animals in a corn producing state? Note the "slit eye" in the large pig. It was advertised in an 1896 price list as a "blind pig." Attention to realism in the old making process is apparent in all Red Wing animals. $400.00-450.00 ea.

Animal bottles are an old and rare part of the American stoneware tradition. Red Wing continued this tradition with this pig bottle. It is both unusual and rare. $550.00-600.00.

The crudely made base on which this pig and piglets rest, the haphazardly painted spots, and the "H. Darling, Red Wing, Minn. April 1, 1893" scratched into the base bottom indicate that this truly was a "lunch hour" piece. $3,500.00-4,000.00.

Individual work and attention to detail were qualities that were often lacking in the era of mass-produced stoneware. Spots on these pigs, however, were meticulously applied and the animals were carefully placed in and around the feeding trough. Were they simply a gift for someone special or were they mass produced this way? $3,000.00-3,500.00.

The stoneware companies of Red Wing produced an array of standing cow and calf statues. Each demostrated a simple elegance and each had its own personality due to the particular potter's skill and/or inclination. $700.00-800.00.

Again, the pose on these beauties is similar, but notice how the base was made to look like natural ground. Too, the unique black spots on a white mother and calf have turned them into Holsteins — very original. $1,200.00-1,500.00

If one is good, two must be better, as demostrated here by the graceful set of two cows and calves on one base — another ingenious variation. $2,000.00-2,500.00.

This cow and calf are in a similar pose, but the big difference from those above is that they are standing on a signed pedestal! Signed animals of any kind are almost impossible to find. $1,500.00-2,000.00.

Other Unique Rarities

It's difficult to believe that the same company which made utilitarian items such as chicken feeders and spittoons could also produce something as delicate and fragile as this. Perhaps, however, the "company" didn't and an individual potter did. Certainly some of the component parts of this statue were molded; yet, of the half dozen or so that are known, each is uniquely different. The crocks that are held by the various boys are undeniably Red Wing in design. Though little else is known about these pieces, there is no denying their beauty, desirability or rarity. $3,0000.00-3,500.00.

Yet another Red Wing industry is immortalized here — the Red Wing Brewery Co. This gorgeous piece demonstrates that many potters were not merely skilled clay workers but truly artists as well. The detailing, glazing, and originality are, without question, unequaled. $3,000.00-3,500.00.

The similiarity of this piece to the Old Sleepy Eye steins made by the Weir Pottery Co. in the very early 1900's causes one to speculate that a Weir potter went to work for Red Wing Stoneware Co. and took his mold with him. All of the known examples (and they are few) are individualized in glazing, mold tooling, and most importantly, by the handwritten personalized messages. The only other writing on this piece is "Best Regard's" (sic). $2,800.00-3,000.00.

The handle disappeared and the stein's top was cut off in order to make this vase or glass. It is, however, from the same mold as the previous stein. Chief Red Wing has, additionally, been given a different colored shirt and tie. "Roxie" is written on this piece as well as the word "Camp." $2,800.00-3,000.00.

Ingenuity at its height is evidenced here. The stein has again been transformed — only this time into a teapot. The opposite side is emblazoned with the word "Mother." Another such "Xmas 1904" teapot is known with the name "Theresa" added. Don't you wish that the potter of these pieces was among **your** ancestors? $3,000.00-3,500.00.

141

The 1901 assassination of President McKinley thrust the nation into deep mourning and caused many types of commemorative tributes to be made in all kinds of mediums. This stoneware bust is perhaps the most elegant. $350.00-450.00.

Flower pots were always big sellers for the stoneware companies, so what better product to be used on this Red Wing Stoneware Co. advertising ashtray than this adorable miniature. Other examples have been found with a miniature crock used in place of the flower pot. $300.00-350.00.

CHAPTER IV: Pottery Era Collectibles

The Red Wing Pottery Co. made a number of signs to advertise their wares which have become collectibles in themselves. The delightful example above advertises art pottery and was designed to be used as part of a store display. It measures 9½" long and 10" tall. The "True China" signs below promoted a new dinnerware line introduced in 1960. They were made in various colors. Top, $700.00-800.00; Bottom, $125.00-150.00.

What better way to advertise the Red Wing pottery industry than to make an ashtray in the form of the familiar wing trademark? Most were red, but once in a while, a lucky collector might find one of a different color. Generally, there are three markings on the bottom, with the 1953 "Anniversary" tray being the most desirable. "Anniversary" $50.00-60.00; Others $35.00-45.00.

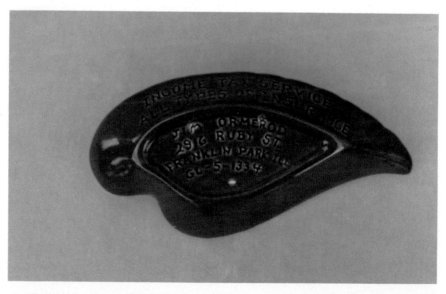

Since the original Red Wing ashtrays were well received by the public, it only makes sense that someone else would want to use them for advertising. $125.00-150.00.

Perhaps the most beautiful and sought after ashtray is what is traditionally called "Pretty Red Wing." Depicted is an Indian maiden in a gracefully sculptured wing. $200.00-250.00.

A round ashtray serves as the second style used to celebrate the 75th anniversary of the Red Wing company in 1953. Note that the embossed items represent those items that the potteries had long been known for — crocks, jugs, and pots as well as the new dinnerware lines. $150.00-200.00.

The Red Wing Pottery Co. was commissioned to make ashtrays to commemorate many different occasions (bridge dedications, bank anniversaries, and hospital openings, to name a few). Among the most memorable, and most collectible, are those made to celebrate the victorious 1965 Minnesota Twins. These three ashtrays first encouraged the Twins to "Win" (top); next, commemorated the All Star Game with a tray in the shape of "home plate" (bottom left); and last, celebrated their making it all the way to the World Series (bottom right). Top, $125.00-175.00; Bottom, L. $225.00-275.00; R. $100.00-125.00.

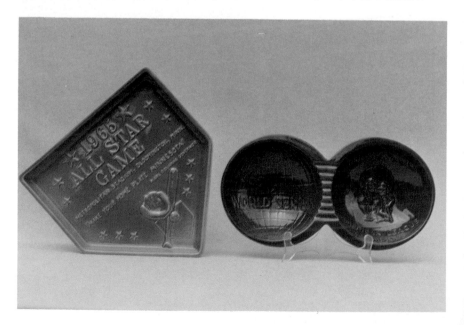

"Ash receivers" were apparently popular items made by many pottery companies. Cigarette ashes were kept and then used to fertilize household plants! The lower bottom numbers indicate that the elephant and donkey were the first two produced, then the dog and cat, and last, the fish and pelican. They each came in a variety of colors, making them cute items and future collectibles. $60.00-80.00 ea.

Having been in existence in St. Paul since 1857, the Hamm's Brewing Co. reached its height in the 1950's. They commissioned the Red Wing Potteries to produce several different premiums which are now very collectible. Among them were these mugs of differing sizes embossed with the words "Hamm's Krug Klub." $60.00-80.00 ea.

The prettiest and rarest of all the Hamm's pieces is probably this large hand-painted salad bowl. It is a piece from a limited edition dinnerware set made for the brewery. The scene depicts the beauty of an idealized Minnesota lake. Hamm's capitalized on this image in their advertising. $175.00-225.00.

This large Hamm's bear bank was made by the thousands at the potteries in the early 1960's. The "land of sky blue waters" used in the familiar Hamm's motto was actually a translation of the Sioux Indian name for this area along the upper Mississippi River. The Hamm's Brewery was sold to the Olympia Brewery Co. in 1975 after having been in existence for over 100 years. $225.00-275.00.

When the demand for crock and jug production declined in the late 1920's, new products and new markets had to be found. It was natural for the stoneware companies to turn to decorative artware lines. This original ad shows samples of the new "brushware" line.

Three different vase shapes and two different stains (blue-green and green) are illustrated here. Acorns, cattails, and flowers were commonly used to decorate pieces from this line. $50.00-60.00 ea.

One of the most attractive and elaborate brushware vases is this tall "cherub" example. Even in 1931 these urns were not cheap as they sold for $30.00 per dozen. (RWU 2) $100.00-125.00.

This very large bread crock is embossed with beautiful sheaves of wheat. Unlike most other brushware pieces, it had a clear (or luster) glaze applied over the outer surface in order to give it a shiny appearance. A small hole in the back allowed humidity to escape when covered with an original lid (not shown). $500.00-600.00.

Besides art ware, dinnerware became a staple product for Red Wing Potteries from the late 1930's until 1967 when they closed. Illustrated here are only a few representative patterns. The most successful pattern ever produced was "Bob White" introduced in 1956 (above.) Most Red Wing dinnerware was hand painted, and the "Tampico" pattern (below left) required 150 brush strokes. Many patterns, for economical reasons, shared the same molds.

Still another mold design was created for these later patterns (above) in the 1960's. Their simple, stylized designs contrast sharply with the ornate and detailed patterns on the previous page. The "Village Green" line shown below was introduced in 1953 and is probably the second most popular pattern made. Its solid colors provide yet another interesting contrast.

Red Wing Stoneware Co. 1877–1906

RW 1

RW 2

RW 3

RW 4

RW 5

RW 6

RW 7

RW 8

RW 9

RW 10

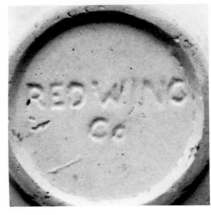

RW 11

RW 12

Minnesota Stoneware Co. 1883–1906

M 1

M 4

M 2

M 5

M 3

M 6

M 7

M 8

M 9

M 10

M 11

M 12

Red Wing Union Stoneware Co. 1906–1936

RWU 1

RWU 2

RWU 3

RWU 4

RWU 5

Red Wing Potteries
1936–1967

RWP 1

Index

Schroeder's
ANTIQUES
Price Guide . . . is the #1 best-selling
antiques & collectibles value guide on the market today,
and here's why . . .

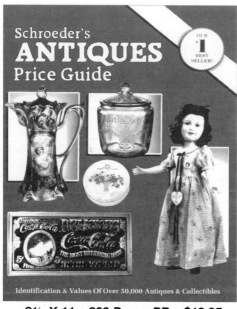
• *More than 300 advisors, well-known dealers, and top-notch collectors work together with our editors to bring you accurate information regarding pricing and identification.*

• *More than 45,000 items in almost 500 categories are listed along with hundreds of sharp original photos that illustrate not only the rare and unusual, but the common, popular collectibles as well.*

• *Each large close-up shot shows important details clearly. Every subject is represented with histories and background information, a feature not found in any of our competitors' publications.*

• *Our editors keep abreast of newly developing trends, often adding several new categories a year as the need arises.*

If it merits the interest of today's collector, you'll find it in *Schroeder's.* And you can feel confident that the information we publish is up to date and accurate. Our advisors thoroughly check each category to spot inconsistencies, listings that may not be entirely reflective of market dealings, and lines too vague to be of merit. Only the best of the lot remains for publication.

Without doubt, you'll find
**SCHROEDER'S ANTIQUES
PRICE GUIDE**
the only one to buy for
reliable information and values.

COLLECTOR BOOKS
A Division of Schroeder Publishing Co., Inc.